SEASCAPE

A PLAY

EDWARD ALBEE

SEASCAPE

A PLAY

NEW YORK 1975

ATHENEUM

FOR

Ella Winter

AND

Donald Ogden Stewart

WITH LOVE

The first performance of SEASCAPE was presented by
RICHARD BARR, CHARLES WOODWARD, and
CLINTON WILDER on Sunday, January 26, 1975, at
the Sam S. Shubert Theatre, New York City.

NANCY	Deborah Kerr
CHARLIE	Barry Nelson
LESLIE	Frank Langella
SARAH	Maureen Anderman

Directed by EDWARD ALBEE

Scenery and Lighting by JAMES STILTON

Costumes by FRED VOELPEL

General Manager, MICHAEL KASDAN

Production Stage Manager, MARK WRIGHT

ACT ONE

The curtain rises. NANCY *and* CHARLIE *on a sand dune. Bright sun. They are dressed informally. There is a blanket and a picnic basket. Lunch is done;* NANCY *is finishing putting things away. There is a pause and then a jet plane is heard from stage right to stage left— growing, becoming deafeningly loud, diminishing.*

NANCY

Such noise they make.

CHARLIE

They'll crash into the dunes one day. I don't know what good they do.

NANCY

(*Looks toward the ocean; sighs*)
Still . . . Oh, Charlie, it's so nice! Can't we stay here forever? Please!

CHARLIE

Unh-unh.

NANCY

That is not why. That is merely no.

CHARLIE

Because.

NANCY

Nor is that.

CHARLIE

Because . . . because you don't really mean it.

NANCY

I do!

CHARLIE

Here?

NANCY (*Expansive*)

Yes!

CHARLIE

Right here on the beach. Build a . . . a tent, or a lean-to.

NANCY (*Laughs gaily*)

No, silly, not this very spot! But *here,* by the shore.

CHARLIE

You wouldn't like it.

NANCY

I would! I'd love it here! I'd love it right where we are, for that matter.

CHARLIE

Not after a while you wouldn't.

NANCY

Yes, I *would*. I love the water, and I love the air, and the sand and the dunes and the beach grass, and the sunshine on all of it and the white clouds way off, and the sunsets and the noise the shells make in the waves and, oh, I love every bit of it, Charlie.

CHARLIE

You wouldn't. Not after a while.

NANCY

Why wouldn't I? I don't even mind the flies and the little . . . sand fleas, I guess they are.

CHARLIE

It gets cold.

NANCY

When?

CHARLIE

In the winter. In the fall even. In spring.

NANCY (*Laughs*)

Well, I don't mean this one, literally . . . not all the
time. I mean go from beach to beach . . . live by the
water. Seaside nomads, that's what we'd be.

CHARLIE

(*Curiously hurt feelings*)
For Christ's sake, Nancy!

NANCY

I mean it! Lord above! There's nothing binding us; you
hate the city . . .

CHARLIE

No.

NANCY (*Undaunted*)

It would be so lovely. Think of all the beaches we could
see.

CHARLIE

No, now . . .

NANCY

Southern California, and the Gulf, and Florida . . . and

up to Maine, and what's-her-name's—Martha's—Vine-
yard, and all those places that the fancy people go: the
Riviera and that beach in Rio de Janeiro, what is that?

CHARLIE

The Copacabana.

NANCY

Yes, and Pago Pago, and . . . Hawaii! Think, Charlie!
We could go around the world and never leave the
beach, just move from one hot sand strip to another: all
the birds and fish and seaside flowers, and all the won-
drous people that we'd meet. Oh, say you'd like to do it,
Charlie.

CHARLIE

No.

NANCY

Just *say* you'd like to.

CHARLIE

If I did you'd say I meant it; you'd hold me to it.

NANCY (*Transparent*)

No I wouldn't. Besides, you have to be pushed into everything.

CHARLIE

Um-hum. But I'm not going to be pushed into . . . into
this—this new business.

NANCY (*Private rapture*)

One great seashore after another; pounding waves and quiet coves; white sand, and red—and black, somewhere, I remember reading; palms, and pine trees, cliffs and reefs, and miles of jungle, sand dunes . . .

CHARLIE

No.

NANCY

. . . and all the people! Every . . . language . . . every . . . race.

CHARLIE

Unh-unh.

NANCY

Of course, I'd never push you.

CHARLIE

You? Never!

NANCY (*Gay*)

Well, maybe a hint here; hint there.

CHARLIE

Don't even do that, hunh?

NANCY

That's all it takes: figure out what you'd really like—
what you want without knowing it, what would secretly
please you, put it in your mind, then make all the plans.
You do it; you like it.

CHARLIE (*Final*)

Nancy, I don't want to travel from beach to beach, cliff
to sand dune, see the races, count the flies. Anything. I
don't want to do . . . anything.

NANCY (*Testy*)

I see. Well.

CHARLIE

I'm happy . . . doing . . . nothing.

NANCY

(*Makes to gather some of their things*)
Well then, we'd best get started. Up! Let's get back!

CHARLIE (*Not moving*)

I just . . . want . . . to . . . do . . . nothing.

NANCY (*Gathering*)

Well, you're certainly not going to do that.
    (*Takes something from him, a pillow, perhaps*)
Hurry now; let's get things together.

CHARLIE (*Aware*)

What . . . Nancy, what on earth are you . . .

NANCY (*Busy*)

We are *not* going to be around forever, Charlie, and you may *not* do nothing. If you don't want to do what *I* want to do—which doesn't matter—then we will do what *you* want to do, but we will not do nothing. We will do *something*. So, tell me what it is you want to do and . . .

CHARLIE

I *said*. Now give me back my . . .

NANCY

You said, "I just want to do nothing; I'm happy doing nothing." Yes? But is that what we've . . . come all this way for?
(*Some wonder and chiding*)
Had the children? Spent all this time together? All the sharing? For nothing? To lie back down in the crib again? The same at the end as at the beginning? Sleep? Pacifier? Milk? Incomprehensible once more?
(*Pause*)
Sleep?
(*Pause*)
Sleep, Charlie? Back to sleep?

CHARLIE

Well, we've earned a little . . .

NANCY

. . . rest.

(*Nods, sort of bitterly*)

We've earned a little rest. Well, why don't we act like the old folks, why don't we sell off, and take one bag apiece and go to California, or in the desert where they have the farms—the retirement farms, the old folks' cities? Why don't we settle in to waiting, like . . . like the camels that we saw in Egypt—groan down on all fours, sigh, and eat the grass, or whatever it is. Why don't we go and wait the judgment with our peers? Take our teeth out, throw away our corset, give in to the palsy, let our mind go dim, play lotto and canasta with the widows and the widowers, eat cereal . . .

(CHARLIE *sighs heavily, exasperatedly*)

Yes! Sigh! Go on! But once you get there, once you *do* that, there's no returning, that purgatory *before* purgatory. No thank you, sir! I haven't come this long way.

CHARLIE

(*Chuckles a little, resigned*)

What do you want to do, Nancy?

NANCY

Nor have you! Not this long way to let loose. All the wisdom—by accident, by accident, some of it—all the wisdom and the . . . unfettering. My God, Charlie: See Everything Twice!

CHARLIE (*Settling back*)

What do you want to do?

NANCY

You are *not* going to live forever, to coin a phrase. Nor
am I, I suppose, come to think of it, though it would be
nice. Nor do I imagine we'll have the satisfaction of
doing it together—head-on with a bus, or into a moun-
tain with a jet, or buried in a snowslide, if we ever *get* to
the Alps. No. I suppose I'll do the tag without you.
Selfish, aren't you—right to the end.

CHARLIE

(*Feeling for her hand, taking it*)
What do you want to do?

NANCY (*Wistful*)

If you get badly sick I'll poison myself.
               (*Waits for reaction, gets none*)
And you?

CHARLIE (*Yawning*)

Yes; if you get badly sick I'll poison *my*self, too.

NANCY

Yes, but then if I *did* take poison, you'd get well again,
and there I'd be, laid out, all for a false alarm. I think
the only thing to do is to *do* something.

CHARLIE (*Nice*)

What would you like to do?

NANCY (*Far away*)

Hm?

CHARLIE

Move from one sand strip to another? Live by the sea
from now on?

NANCY (*Great wistfulness*)

Well, we have nothing holding us, except together; chattel? Does chattel mean what I think it does? We *have*
nothing we *need* have. We could do it; I would so like
to.

CHARLIE (*Smiles*)

All right.

NANCY (*Sad little laugh*)

You're humoring me; it *is* something I want, though;
maybe only the principle.
      (*Larger laugh*)
I suspect our children would have us put away if we an-
nounced it as a plan—beachcombing, leaf huts. Even if
we did it in hotels they'd have a case—for our *reasons.*

CHARLIE

Mmmmmmm.

NANCY

Let's merely have it for today . . . and tomorrow, and

. . . who knows: continue the temporary and it becomes
forever.

CHARLIE (*Relaxed; content*)

All right.
    (*The sound of the jet plane from stage right to
    stage left—growing, becoming deafeningly
    loud, diminishing*)

NANCY

Such noise they make!

CHARLIE

They'll crash into the dunes one day; I don't know what
good they do.

NANCY (*After a pause*)

Still . . . Ahhh; breathe the sea air.
    (*Tiny pause; suddenly remembers*)
Didn't you tell me? When you were a little boy you
wanted to live in the sea?

CHARLIE

Under.

NANCY (*Delighted*)

Yes! Under the water—in it. That all your friends pined
to have wings? Icarus? Soar?

CHARLIE

But not too near the sun; and real wings, not pasted on.

NANCY

Yes, but you wanted to go under. Gills, too?

CHARLIE

As I remember. A regular fish, I mean fishlike—arms and
legs and everything, but able to go under, live down in
the coral and the ferns, come home for lunch and bed
and stories, of course, but down in the green, the purple,
and big enough not to be eaten if I stayed close in. Oh
yes; I *did* want that.

NANCY

(*Considers it, with some wonder*)
Be a fish.
(*Lightly*)
No, that's not among what *I* wanted—when *I* was little,
not that I remember. I wanted to be a pony once, I
think, but not for very long. I wanted to be a *woman*. I
wanted to grow up to be *that*, and all it had with it.
(*Notices something below her in the distance,
upstage. Offhand*)
There are some people down there; I thought we were
alone. In the water; some people, I think.
(*Back*)
And, I suppose I *have* become that.

CHARLIE (*Smiling*)

You have.

NANCY

In any event, the appearances of it: husband, children—
precarious, those, for a while, but nicely settled now—to
all appearances—and the grandchildren . . . here, and
on the way. The top of the pyramid! Us two, the children, and all of theirs.
(*Mildly puzzled*)
Isn't it odd that you can build a pyramid from the top
down? Isn't that difficult? The engineering?

CHARLIE

There wasn't anyone before us?

NANCY (*Laughs lightly*)

Well, yes, but everybody builds his own, starts fresh,
starts up in the air, builds the base around him. Such
levitation! Our own have started *theirs*.

CHARLIE

It's all one.

NANCY (*Sort of sad about it*)

Yes.
(*Bright again*)
Or maybe it's the most . . . difficult, the most . . .
breathtaking of all: the whole thing balanced on one

point; a reversed *pyramid*, always in danger of toppling
over when people don't behave themselves.

CHARLIE (*Chuckling*)

All right.

NANCY (*Above it*)

You have no interest in imagery. None.

CHARLIE (*Defiance; rue*)

Well, I used to.

NANCY

The man who married a dumb wife; not you! Was that
Molière? Beaumarchais?

CHARLIE

Anatole France.

NANCY

Was it?

CHARLIE

(*Continuing from before*)

I used to go way down; at our summer place; a protected
cove. The breakers would come in with a storm, or a
high wind, but not usually. I used to go way down, and
try to stay. I remember before that, when I was tiny, I
would go in the swimming pool, at the shallow end, let

out my breath and sit on the bottom; when you let out your breath—all of it—you sink, gently, and you can sit on the bottom until your lungs need air. I would do that —I was so young—sit there, gaze about. Great trouble for my parents. "Good God, go get Charlie; he's gone and sunk again." "Will you look at that child? Put him in the water and he drops like a stone." I could swim perfectly well, as easy as walking, and around the same time, but I used to love to sink. And when I was older, we were by the sea. Twelve; yes, or thirteen. I used to lie on the warm boulders, strip off . . .

(Quiet, sad amusement)

. . . learn about my body; no one saw me; twelve or thirteen. And I would go into the water, take two stones, as large as I could manage, swim out a bit, tread, look up one final time at the sky . . . relax . . . begin to go down. Oh, twenty feet, fifteen, soft landing without a sound, the white sand clouding up where your feet touch, and all around you ferns . . . and lichen. You can stay down there so long! You can build it up, and last . . . so long, enough for the sand to settle and the fish come back. And they do—come back—all sizes, some slowly, eyeing past; some streak, and you think for a moment they're larger than they are, sharks, maybe, but they never are, and one stops being an intruder, finally— just one more object come to the bottom, or living thing, part of the undulation and the silence. It was very good.

NANCY

Did the fish talk to you? I mean, did they come up and stay close, and look at you, and maybe nibble at your toes?

CHARLIE (*Very shy*)

Some of them.

NANCY (*Enthusiastic*)

Why don't you go and do it! Yes!

CHARLIE (*Age*)

Oh, no, now, Nancy, I couldn't.

NANCY

Yes! Yes, you could! Go do it again; you'd love it!

CHARLIE

Oh, no, now, I . . .

NANCY

Go down to the edge; go in! Pick up some stones . . .

CHARLIE

There're no coves; it's all open beach.

NANCY

Oh, you'll find a cove; go on! Be young again; my God,
Charlie, be young!

CHARLIE

No; besides, someone'd see me; they'd think I was drowning.

NANCY

Who's to see you?! Look, there's no one in the . . . no, those . . . people, they've come out, the ones were in the water, they're . . . well, they're lying on the beach, to sun; they're prone. Go on down; I'll watch you from here.

CHARLIE
(*Firm, through embarrassment*)
No! I said no!

NANCY
(*Undaunted; still happy*)
Well, I'll come with you; I'll stand by the edge, and if anyone comes by and says, "Look, there's a man drowning!" I'll laugh and say, "La! It's my husband, and he's gone down with two stones to sit on the bottom for a while."

CHARLIE

No!

NANCY

The white sand clouding, and the ferns and the lichen. Oh, do it, Charlie!

CHARLIE

I wouldn't like it any more.

NANCY

(*Wheedling, taunting*)
Awwww, how long since you've done it?!

CHARLIE (*Mumbles*)

Too long.

NANCY

What?

CHARLIE (*Embarrassed; shy*)

Not since I was seventeen?

NANCY

(*This time pretending not to hear*)
What?

CHARLIE

(*Rather savage; phlegm in the throat*)
Too long.
(*Small pause*)
Far too long?
(*Silence*)

NANCY

(*Very gentle; not even urging*)
Would it be so very hard now? Wouldn't you be able
to? Gently? In some sheltered place, not very deep? Go
down? Not long, just enough to . . . reconfirm.

CHARLIE (*Flat*)

I'd rather remember.

NANCY

If *I* were a man—What a silly thing to say.

CHARLIE

Yes. It is.

NANCY

Still, if I were . . . I don't think I'd let the chance go by;
not if I had it.

CHARLIE (*Quietly*)

Let it go.

NANCY

Not if *I* had it. There isn't that much. Sex goes . . .
diminishes; well, it becomes a holiday and rather special,
and not like eating, or going to sleep. But that's nice, too
—that it becomes special—
(*Laughs gaily*)

Do you know, I had a week when I thought of divorcing you?

CHARLIE

(*Quite surprised, vulnerable; shakes his head*)
No.

NANCY

Yes. You were having your thing, your melancholia—poor darling—and there I was, brisk and thirty, still pert, learning the moles on your back instead of your chest hairs.

CHARLIE (*Relieved, if sad*)

Ah. Then.

NANCY (*Nods*)

Um-hum. Then. Rereading Proust, if I have it right. Propped up in bed, all pink and ribbons, smelling good, not all those creams and looking ten years married as I might have, and who would have blamed me, but fresh, and damned attractive, if I have to say it for myself; propped up in bed, literate, sweet-smelling, getting familiar with your back. One, two, three moles, and then a pair of them, twins, flat black ones . . .

CHARLIE (*Recalling*)

That time.

NANCY (*Nods*)

. . . ummmm. The ones I said should go—*still* think

they should—not that it matters: they haven't done anything. It was at the . . . center of your thing, your seven-
month decline; it was *then* that I thought of divorcing
you. The deeper your inertia went, the more *I* felt alive.
Good wife, patient, see him through it, whatever it is,
wonder if it isn't something *you* haven't done, or have;
write home for some advice, but oh, so busy, with the
children and the house. Stay neat; don't pry; weather it.
But right in the center, three and a half months in, it occurred to me that there was nothing wrong, save perhaps
another woman.

CHARLIE (*Surprised; hurt*)

Oh, Nancy.

NANCY

Well, one has a mind, and it goes about its business. If
one is happy, *and* content, it doesn't mean that everyone
else is; never assume that. Maybe he's found a girl; not
even looking, necessarily; maybe he turned a corner one
afternoon and there was a girl, not prettier even, maybe
a little plain, but unencumbered, or lonely, or lost.
That's the way it starts, as often as not. No sudden pas-
sion over champagne glasses at the fancy ball, or seeing
the puppy love again, never like that except for fiction,
but something . . . different, maybe even a little . . .
less: the relief of that; simpler, not quite so nice, how
much nicer, for a little.

CHARLIE

Nothing like that.

NANCY (*Laughs a little*)

Well, *I* know.

CHARLIE

Nothing at *all*.

NANCY

Yes, but the *mind*. And what bothered me was not what *you* might be doing—oh, well, certainly; *bothered*, yes— not entirely what you might be doing, but that, all of a sudden, *I* had not. *Ever*. Had not even thought of it. A child at thirty, I suppose. Without that time I would have gone through my entire life and never thought of another man, another pair of arms, harsh cheek, hard buttocks, pleasure, never at all.
(*Considers that*)
Well, I might have, and maybe this was better. All at once I thought: it was over between us—not our life together, that would go on, and we would be like a minister and his sister—the . . . active part of our life, the rough-and-tumble in the sheets or in the grass when we took our picnics, that all of that had stopped between us, or would become cursory, and I wouldn't have asked why, nor would you have said, or if I *had*—asked why— you would have said some lie, or truth, would have made it worse, and I thought back to before I married you, and the boys I would have done it with, if I had been that type, the firm-fleshed boys I would have taken in my arms had it occurred to me. And I began to think of them, Proust running on, pink and ribbons, looking at your back, and your back would turn and it would be

Johnny Smythe or the Devlin boy, or one of the others, and he would smile, reach out a hand, undo my ribbons, draw me close, ease on. Oh, that was a troubling time.

CHARLIE (*Sad remembrance*)

You were never one for the boys, were you?

NANCY (*She, too*)

No.
(*Pause*)
But I thought: well, if he can turn his back on me like this—nice, isn't it, when the real and the figurative come together—*I* can turn, too—if not my back, then . . . back. I can have me a divorce, I thought, become eighteen again.
(*Sudden thought*)
You know, I think that's why our women want divorces, as often as not—to be eighteen again, no matter how old they are; and daring. To do it differently, and still for the first time.
(*Sighs*)
But it was only a week I thought about that. It went away. You came back . . . eventually.

CHARLIE

(*A statement of fact that is really a question*)
You never thought I went to anyone else.

NANCY

She said to me—wise woman—"Daughter, if it lasts, if

you and he come back together, it'll be at a price or two. If it lasts there'll be accommodation, wandering; if he doesn't do it in the flesh, he'll think about it; one night, in the dark, if you listen hard enough, you'll hear him think the name of another woman, kiss *her*, touch *her* breasts as he has his hand and mouth on you. *Then* you'll know something about loneliness, my daughter; yessiree; you'll be halfway there, halfway to compassion."

CHARLIE (*After a pause; shy*)

The other half?

NANCY

Hm?

(*Matter-of-fact*)

Knowing how lonely *he* is . . . substituting . . . using a person, a body, and wishing it was someone else—almost anyone. *That* void. *Le petit mort*, the French call the moment of climax? And that lovely writer? Who talks of the sadness after love? After intimate intercourse, I think he says? But what of *during*? What of the loneliness and death *then*? *During.* They don't talk of that: the sad fantasies; the substitutions. The thoughts we have.

(*Tiny pause*)

One has.

CHARLIE

(*Softly, with a timid smile*)

I've never been with another woman.

NANCY (*A little laugh*)

Well, *I* know.

CHARLIE (*Laughs ruefully*)

I think one time, when you and I were making love—
when we were nearly there, I remember I pretended it
was a week or so before, one surprising time we'd had,
something we'd hit upon by accident, or decided to do
finally; I pretended it was the time before, and it was
quite good that way.

NANCY (*Some wonder*)

You pretended I was me.

CHARLIE (*Apology*)

Well . . . yes.

NANCY

(*Laughs delightedly; thinks*)
Well; perhaps I was.
(*Pause*)
So much goes, Charlie; we shouldn't give up until we
have to.
(*Gentle*)
Why don't you go down; why don't you find a cove?

CHARLIE

(*Smiles; shakes his head*)
No.

NANCY

It's something *I've* never done; you could teach me. You could take my hand; we could have two big stones, and we could go down together.

CHARLIE

(*Not a complaint; an evasion*)
I haven't got my suit.

NANCY

Go bare! You're quite presentable.

CHARLIE

Nancy!
        (*Mildly put off, and a little pleased*)

NANCY (*Almost shy*)

I wouldn't mind. I'd like to see you, pink against the blue, watch the water on you.

CHARLIE

Tomorrow.

NANCY

Bare?

CHARLIE

We'll see.

NANCY (*Shrugs*)

I'm used to that: we'll see, and then put off until it's for-gotten.

(*Peers*)

I wonder where they've gone.

CHARLIE

(*Not interested*)

Who?

NANCY

Those people; well, those that were down there.

CHARLIE

Gone in.

NANCY

The water? Again?

CHARLIE

No. Home.

NANCY

Well, I don't think so. I thought maybe they were com-ing up to us.

CHARLIE

Why?

NANCY

They . . . looked to be. I mean, I thought . . . well, no matter.

CHARLIE

Who were they?

NANCY

You know my eyes. I thought they were climbing, coming up to see us.

CHARLIE

If we don't know them?

NANCY

Some people are adventurous.

CHARLIE

Mmmmm.

NANCY

I wonder where they've gone.

CHARLIE

Don't spy!

NANCY (*Looking down*)

I'm not; I just want to . . . Lord, why couldn't my ears be going instead? I think I see them halfway up the dune. I think I can make them out; resting, or maybe sunning, on an angle for the sun.

CHARLIE

A lot of good *you'd* be under water.

NANCY

(*Considers what she has seen*)
Rather odd.
(*Dismisses it*)
Well, that's why you'll have to take me if I'm going to go down; you wouldn't want to lose me in the fernery, and all. An eddy, or whatever that is the tide does underneath, might sweep me into a cave, or a culvert, and I wouldn't know *what* to do. No, you'll have to take me.

CHARLIE

You'd probably panic . . . if I took you under.
(*Thinks about it*)
No; you wouldn't; you'd do worse, most likely: start drowning and not let on.
(*They both laugh*)
You're a good wife.

NANCY (*Offhand*)

You've been a good husband . . . more or less.

CHARLIE (*Not aggressive*)

Damned right.

NANCY

And you courted me the way I wanted.

CHARLIE

Yes.

NANCY

And you gave me the children I wanted, as many, and when.

CHARLIE

Yes.

NANCY

And you've provided a sturdy shoulder and a comfortable life. No?

CHARLIE

Y*es.*

NANCY

And I've not a complaint in my head, have I?

CHARLIE

No.

NANCY (*Slightly bitter*)

Well, we'll wrap you in the flag when you're gone, and
do taps.
(*A fair silence*)

CHARLIE (*Soft; embarrassed*)

We'd better . . . gather up; . . . We should go back
now.

NANCY

(*Nudges him on the shoulder*)
Ohhhhhhhh . . .
(CHARLIE *shakes his head, keeping his eyes
averted.*)

NANCY

Ohhhhhhhhh . . .

CHARLIE

I don't want to stay here any more. You've hurt my feelings, damn it!

NANCY (*Sorry*)

Ohhh, Charlie.

CHARLIE

(*Trying to understand*)
You're not cruel by nature; it's not your way. Why do
you *do* this? Even so rarely; *why?*

NANCY

(*As if it explained everything*)
I was being *pet*ulant.

CHARLIE

(*More or less to himself, but not sotto voce*)
I *have* been a good husband to you; I *did* court you like a
gentleman; I *have* been a good lover . . .

NANCY (*Light*)

Well, of course I have no one to compare you with.

CHARLIE

(*Preoccupied; right on*)
. . . you *have* been comfortable, and my shoulder *has*
been there.

NANCY (*Gaily*)

I *know;* I *know.*

CHARLIE

You've had a good *life.*

NANCY

Don't *say* that!

CHARLIE

And you'll not pack it up in a piece of cloth and put it away.

NANCY

No! Not if *you* won't! Besides, it was hyperbole.

CHARLIE (*Slightly testy*)

I knew that. Not if *I* won't, eh? Not if I won't what?

NANCY

Pack it up in a piece of cloth and put it away. When's the last time you were stung by a bee, Charlie? Was it that time in Maine . . . or Delaware? When your cheek swelled up, and you kept saying, "Mud! Get me some mud!" And there wasn't any mud that *I* could see, and you said, "Well, *make* some."

CHARLIE

Delaware.

NANCY

After all the years of making you things, my mind couldn't focus on how to make *mud*. What *is* the recipe

for *that*, I said to myself . . . What sort of *pan* do I use,
for one; water, yes, but water and . . . what? Earth, naturally, but what *kind* and . . . oh, I felt so foolish.

CHARLIE (*Softer*)

It was Delaware.

NANCY

So foolish.

CHARLIE (*Mildly reproachful*)

The whole cheek swelled up; the eyes was half closed.

NANCY (*Pedagogic*)

Well, that's what a bee sting does, Charlie. And that's
what brings on the petulance—mine; it's just like a bee
sting, and I re*mem*ber, though it's been years.

CHARLIE

(*To reassure himself*)

Crazy as a loon.

NANCY

No; not at all. You asked me about the petulance—why
it comes on me, even rarely. Well, it's like the sting of a
bee: something you say, or do; or don't say, or don't do.
And it brings the petulance on me—that I like it, but it's
a healthy sign, shows I'm still nicely alive.

CHARLIE (*Not too friendly*)

Like when? Like what?

NANCY

What brings it on, and when?

CHARLIE (*Impatient*)

Yes!

NANCY

Well, so many things.

CHARLIE

Give me *one*.

NANCY

No; I'll give you several.

CHARLIE

All *right*.

NANCY

"You've had a good life."

(*Pause*)

CHARLIE (*Curiously angry*)

All right. *Go* on.

NANCY

Do you know what I'm *saying*?

CHARLIE

You're throwing it up to me; you're telling me I've had a
. . .

NANCY

No-no-no! I'm saying what you *said*, what you told *me*.
You told me, you said to me, "You've had a good life." I
wasn't talking about *you*, though you *have*. I was saying
what you said to me.

CHARLIE (*Annoyed*)

Well, you have! You *have* had!

NANCY (*She, too*)

Yes! Have *had*! What *about* that!

CHARLIE

What about it!

NANCY

Am not *having*.
        (*Waits for reaction; gets none*)
Am not *having?* Am not *having* a good life?

CHARLIE

Well, of *course!*

NANCY

Then why say had? Why put it that way?

CHARLIE

It's a way of speaking!

NANCY

No! It's a way of thinking! *I* know the language, and I
know *you.* You're not careless with it, or didn't used to
be. Why *not* go to those places in the desert and let our
heads deflate, if it's all in the past? Why not just *do*
that?

CHARLIE

It was a way of speaking.

NANCY

Dear God, we're *here*. We've served our time, Charlie,
and there's nothing telling us do *that,* or any condi-

tional; not any more. Well, there's the arthritis in my
wrist, of course, and the eyes have known a better sea-
son, and there's always the cancer or a heart attack to
think about if we're bored, but besides all these things
. . . what is there?

CHARLIE (*Somewhat triste*)

You're at it again.

NANCY

I am! Words are lies; they *can* be, and you *use* them, but
I know what's in your gut. I *told* you, didn't I?

CHARLIE (*Passing it off*)

Sure, sure.

NANCY (*Mimicking*)

Sure, sure. Well, they are, and you do. What *have* we
got left?

CHARLIE

What! You mean besides the house, the kids, *their* kids,
friends, all that? What?!

NANCY

Two things!

CHARLIE

Yeah?

NANCY

Ourselves and some time. Charlie—the pyramid's build-
ing by itself; the earth's spinning in its own fashion
without any push from us; we've done all we ought to—
and isn't it splendid we've enjoyed so much of it.

CHARLIE (*Mild irony*)

We're pretty splendid people.

NANCY

Damned right we are, and now we've got each other and
some time, and all *you* want to do is become a vegetable.

CHARLIE

Fair, as usual.

NANCY (*Shrugs*)

All right: a lump.

CHARLIE

We've earned . . .

NANCY (*Nods*)

. . . a little rest. My God, you say that twice a day, and
sometimes in between.
                    (*Mutters*)

We've earned a little *life*, if you ask *me*.
>   (*Pause*)
Ask me.

>   CHARLIE (*Some rue*)
No; you'd tell me.

>   NANCY

>   (*Bold and recriminating*)
Sure! Course I would! When else are we going to get it?

>   CHARLIE

>   (*Quite serious; quite bewildered*)
What's to be gained? And what would we really get?
Some . . . illusion, I suppose; some smoke. There'd be
the same sounds in the dark—or similar ones; we'd have
to sleep and wonder if we'd waken, either way. It's six of
one, except we'll do it on familiar ground, if *I* have *my*
way. I'm not up to the glaciers and the crags, and I don't
think you'd be . . . once you got out there.

>   NANCY (*Grudging*)

I do admit, you make it sound scary—first time away to
camp, sleeping out, the hoot owls and the goblins. Oh,
that's scary. Are you telling me you're all caved in,
Charlie?

>   CHARLIE

>   (*Pause; considers the fact*)
Maybe.

NANCY

(*Pause while she ponders this*)
All closed down? Then . . . what's the difference? You
make it ugly enough, either way. The glaciers and the
crags? At least we've never *tried that.*

CHARLIE

(*Trying to justify, but without much enthusiasm*)
There's comfort in settling in.

NANCY (*Pause*)

Small.

CHARLIE (*Pause, final*)

Some.
(*A silence*)
LESLIE *appears, upper half of trunk pops up upstage, from behind the dune. Neither* CHARLIE
nor NANCY *sees him.* LESLIE *looks at the two of
them, pops back down out of sight*)

NANCY

(*To bring them back to life again*)
Well. I've got to do some postcards tonight; tell all the
folks where we are.

CHARLIE

Yes?

NANCY

. . . what a time we're having. I've got a list . . . somewhere. It wouldn't be nice not to. They do it for us, and
it's such fun getting them.

CHARLIE

Um-hum.

NANCY

You do some, too?

CHARLIE

You do them for both of us.

NANCY (*Mildly disappointed*)

Oh.

(*Pause*)

All right.

CHARLIE (*Not very interested*)

What do you want to do, then?

NANCY

(*While* NANCY *speaks,* LESLIE *and* SARAH *come
up on the dune, behind* CHARLIE *and* NANCY,
*but some distance away. They crawl up; then
they squat down on their tails.* NANCY
stretches)

Oh, I don't know. Do you want to have your nap? Cover
your face if you do, though; put something on it. *Or . . .*
we could go on back. *Or . . .* we *could* do a stroll down
the beach. If you won't go in, we'll find some pretty shells
. . . I will.

CHARLIE (*Small smile*)

What a wealth.

NANCY (*Fairly cheerful*)

Well . . . we make the best of it.
    (CHARLIE *senses something behind him. He
turns his head, sees* LESLIE *and* SARAH. *His
mouth falls open; he is stock-still for a moment; then, slowly getting on all fours, he
begins, very cautiously, to back away.* NANCY
sees what CHARLIE *is doing, is momentarily
puzzled. Then she looks behind her. She sees*
LESLIE *and* SARAH)

NANCY

(*Straightening her back abruptly*)
My goodness!

CHARLIE

(*On all fours; ready to flee*)
Ohmygod.

NANCY (*Great wonder*)

Charlie!

CHARLIE

(*Eyes steady on* LESLIE AND SARAH)
Oh my loving God.

NANCY (*Enthusiasm*)

Charlie! What *are* they?!

CHARLIE

Nancy, get back here!

NANCY

But, Charlie . . .

CHARLIE

(*Deep in his throat; trying to whisper*)
Get back here!
  (NANCY *backs away until she and* CHARLIE *are
  together.*)

  NOTE: CHARLIE *and* NANCY *are now toward
  stage right,* LESLIE *and* SARAH *toward stage left.
  They will not hear each other speak until in-
  dicated.*

  (*Whispering*)
Get a stick!

NANCY (*Interest and wonder*)

Charlie, what are they?

CHARLIE (*Urgent*)

Get me a stick!

NANCY

A what?

CHARLIE (*Louder*)

A stick!

NANCY

(*Looking about; uncertain*)
Well . . . what *sort* of stick, Charlie?

CHARLIE

A stick! A wooden *stick!*

NANCY

(*Begins to crawl stage right*)
Well, of course a wooden stick, Charlie; what other
kinds of sticks *are* there, for heaven's sake? But what sort
of stick?

CHARLIE

(*Never taking his eyes off* LESLIE *and* SARAH)
A big one! A big stick!

NANCY

(*None too happy about it*)
Well . . . I'll *look*. Driftwood, I suppose . . .

CHARLIE

Well, of course a *wooden* stick, Charlie; what other
kinds of sticks . . .
    (LESLIE *moves a little, maybe raises an arm*)
GET ME A GUN!

NANCY (*Astonished*)

A *gun*, Charlie! Where on earth would anyone find a
gun up here.

CHARLIE (*Shrill*)

Get me a stick!

NANCY (*Cross*)

All right!

CHARLIE

    (SARAH *moves toward* LESLIE; CHARLIE *stiffens,*
    gasps)
Hurry!

NANCY

I'm looking!

CHARLIE

(*A bleak fact, to himself as much as anything*)
They're going to come at us, Nancy . . .
                    (*An afterthought*)
. . . , and we're arguing.

NANCY

(*Waving a smallish stick; thin, crooked, eighteen inches, maybe*)
I found one, Charlie; Charlie, I found one!

CHARLIE

(*Not taking his gaze off* LESLIE *and* SARAH; *between his teeth*)
Well, bring it here.

NANCY

(*Crawling to* CHARLIE *with the stick between
her teeth*)
It's the best I could do under the circumstances. There
was a big trunk or something . . .

CHARLIE (*His hand out*)

Give it to me!

NANCY

Here!

(*Gives the stick to* CHARLIE, *who, without
looking at it, raises it in his right hand*)
Charlie! They're magnificent!

CHARLIE

(*Realizes what he is brandishing, looks at it
with distaste and loss*)
What's *this*?

NANCY

It's your stick.

CHARLIE (*Almost crying*)

Oh my God.

NANCY

(*Eyes on* LESLIE *and* SARAH)
Charlie, I think they're absolutely beautiful. What *are*
they?

CHARLIE

What am I supposed to *do* with it?!

NANCY

You *asked* for it, Charlie; you said you wanted it.

CHARLIE

(*Snorts: ironic-pathetic*)
Go down fighting, eh?

(LESLIE *clears his throat; it is a large sound,
rather like a growl or a bark. Instinctively,*
CHARLIE *gathers* NANCY *to him, all the while
trying to brandish his stick*)

NANCY

(*Not at all sure of herself*)
Fight, Charlie? Fight? Are they going to hurt us?

CHARLIE

(*Laughing at the absurdity*)
Oh, God!

NANCY (*More vigor*)

Well, at least we'll be together.
(LESLIE *clears his throat again, same sound;*
CHARLIE *and* NANCY *react a little, tense.* LESLIE
*takes a step forward, stops, bends over and
picks up a large stick, four feet long and stout;
he brandishes it and clears his throat again*)
Now, *that's* an impressive stick.

CHARLIE

(*Shakes his stick at her*)
Yeah; thanks.

NANCY (*Some pique*)

Well, thank *you* very much. If I'd known I was supposed to go over there and crawl around under their
flippers, or pads, or whatever they have . . .

CHARLIE

(*Final words; some haste*)
I love you, Nancy.

NANCY

(*The tiniest pause; a trifle begrudging*)
Well . . . I love *you*, too.
(LESLIE *slowly, so slowly, raises his stick above
him in a gesture of such strength that should
he smite the earth it would tremble. He holds
the stick thus, without moving*)

CHARLIE

Well, I certainly hope so: here they come.
(LESLIE *and* SARAH *slowly begin to move toward* CHARLIE *and* NANCY. *Suddenly the sound
of the jet plane again, lower and louder this
time.* LESLIE *and* SARAH *react as animals would;
frozen for an instant, tense seeking of the
danger, poised, every muscle taut, and then the
two of them, at the same instant and with
identical movement—paws clawing at the sand,
bellies hugging the earth—they race back over
the dune toward the water.*
CHARLIE *and* NANCY *are as if struck dumb; they
stare, open-mouthed, at the now-vacated dune*)

NANCY

(*Finally, with great awe*)

Charlie!

(*Infinite wonder*)

What have we *seen?!*

CHARLIE

The glaciers and the crags, Nancy. You'll never be closer.

NANCY

All at *once!* There they *were,* Charlie!

CHARLIE

It was the liver paste. That explains everything.

NANCY (*Tolerant smile*)

Yes; certainly.

CHARLIE

I'm sure it was the liver paste. I knew it. When you were packing the lunch this morning, I said what is that? And you said it's liver paste, for sandwiches; what's the matter, don't you like liver paste any more? And I said what do we need *that* for? For sandwiches, you said. And I said yes, but what do we *need* it for?

NANCY

But, Charlie . . .

CHARLIE

You've got a roasted chicken there, and peaches, and a brie, and bread and wine, what do we need the sandwiches for, the liver paste?

NANCY

You might want them, I said.

CHARLIE

But, with all the rest.

NANCY

Besides, I asked you what would happen if you picked up the roasted chicken and dropped it in the sand. What would you do—rinse it off with the wine? Then I'd have to make iced tea, too. Miles up on the dunes, no fresh water anywhere? Bring a thermos of iced tea, too, in case you dropped the chicken in the sand?

CHARLIE

When have I dropped a chicken in the sand? *When* have I done that?

NANCY (*Mildly piqued*)

I wasn't suggesting it was a thing you *did*; I wasn't pointing to a history of it; I said you *might*. But, Charlie . . . at a time like *this* . . . they may come back.

CHARLIE

Liver paste doesn't keep; I *told* you that: goes bad in a minute, with the heat and all.

NANCY

Wrapped up in silver foil.

CHARLIE

Aluminum.

NANCY

. . . whatever; wrapped up and perfectly safe, it keeps.

CHARLIE

It goes bad in a minute, which is what it did: the liver paste clearly went bad. It went bad in the sun and it poisoned us.

NANCY

(*Sees* SARAH *in the distance, or thinks she does*)
Pardon?

CHARLIE (*Dogmatic; glum*)

It went bad, as I said it would: the liver paste, for all your wrapping up. It went bad, and it poisoned us; *that's* what happened!

NANCY

Poisoned us?!
            (*Disbelieving, and distracted*)
And *then* what happened?

CHARLIE

        (*Looks at her as if she's simple-minded*)
Why . . . we *died*, of course.

NANCY

We died?

CHARLIE

We ate the liver paste and we died. That drowsy feeling
. . . the sun . . . and the wine . . . none of it: all those
night thoughts of what it would be like, the sudden
scalding in the center of the chest, or wasting away; milk
in the eyes, voices from the other room; none of it. Chew
your warm sandwich, wash it down, lie back, and let the
poison have its way . . .
        (LESLIE *and* SARAH *reappear over the dune; for-
        midable, upright.* NANCY *begins laughing*)
. . . talk—*think* you're talking—and all the while the
cells are curling up, disconnecting . . . Nancy, don't do
that! . . . it all goes dim . . . Don't laugh at me! . . .
and then you're dead.
        (*Between her bursts of laughter*)
How can you *do* that?
        (LESLIE *and* SARAH *move toward* CHARLIE *and*
        NANCY, *cautiously and intimidatingly;* NANCY

*sees them, points, and her laughter changes its
quality*)

How can you laugh when you're dead, Nancy? Now,
don't *do* that!

NANCY

We may be dead already, Charlie, but I think we're
going to die again. Here they come!

CHARLIE

Oh my *dear* God!
(LESLIE *and* SARAH *approach, but stop a fair
distance away from* CHARLIE *and* NANCY; *they
are on their guard*)

NANCY (*After a pause*)

Charlie, there's only one thing for it. Watch me now;
watch me carefully.

CHARLIE

Nancy . . .
(*She smiles broadly; with her feet facing*
LESLIE *and* SARAH, *she slowly rolls over on her
back, her legs drawn up, her hands by her face,
fingers curved, like paws. She holds this position, smiling broadly*)

NANCY

Do *this*, Charlie! For God's sake, do *this*!

CHARLIE (*Confused*)

Nancy . . .

NANCY

It's called "submission," Charlie! I've seen it in the books. I've read how the animals do it. Do it, Charlie! Roll over! Please!
(CHARLIE *hesitates a moment, looks at* LESLIE *and* SARAH)
Do it, Charlie!
(*Slowly,* CHARLIE *smiles broadly at* LESLIE *and* SARAH, *assumes* NANCY's *position*)

CHARLIE (*Finally*)

All right.

NANCY

Now, Charlie, smile! And mean it!

CURTAIN

ACT TWO

ACT TWO

The curtain rises. The set: the same as the end of ACT ONE. CHARLIE, NANCY, LESLIE, *and* SARAH *as they were. All are stock-still for a moment.*

LESLIE

(*Turns his head toward* SARAH)
Well, Sarah, what do you think?

SARAH (*Shakes her head*)
I don't know, Leslie.

LESLIE

What do you think they're doing?

SARAH

Well, it *looks* like some sort of a submission pose, but you never know; it might be a trick.

LESLIE

I'll take a look.

SARAH

Well, be very careful.

LESLIE (*A weary sigh*)

Yes, Sarah.

(LESLIE *starts moving over to where* CHARLIE
and NANCY *lie in their submission postures*)

CHARLIE

Oh my God, one of them's coming.

NANCY

Stay very still.

CHARLIE

What if one of them touches me?

NANCY

Smile.

CHARLIE

I'll scream.

NANCY

No, don't do *that*.

CHARLIE

(*Whispers out of the side of his mouth*)
It's coming! It's coming!

NANCY

Well . . . hold on, and don't panic. If we had a tail,
this'd be the perfect time to wag it.
(LESLIE *is very close*)

CHARLIE

Oh, God.
(LESLIE *stops, leans forward toward* CHARLIE,
*and sniffs him several times. Then he
straightens up and pokes* CHARLIE *in the ribs
with his footpaw.* CHARLIE *makes an involun-
tary sound but holds his position and keeps
smiling.* LESLIE *looks at* NANCY, *sniffs her a little, and pokes her, too. She holds her position
and wags her hands a little.* LESLIE *surveys
them both, then turns and ambles back to*
SARAH)

SARAH

Well?

LESLIE

Well . . . they don't look very . . . formidable—in the
sense of prepossessing. Not young. They've got their
teeth bared, but they don't look as though they're going
to bite. Their hide is funny—feels soft.

SARAH

How do they smell?

LESLIE

Strange.

SARAH

Well, I should suppose *so*.

LESLIE (*Not too sure*)

I guess it's *safe*.

SARAH

Are you *sure?*

LESLIE (*Laughs a little*)

No; of course not.
            (*Scratches his head*)

NANCY (*Sotto voce*)

What are they doing?

CHARLIE

It poked me; one of them poked me; I thought it was all
over.

NANCY (*Not to be left out*)

Well, it poked *me*, too.

CHARLIE

It *sniffed* at *me.*

NANCY

Yes. Keep where you are, Charlie; don't move. It sniffed at *me,* too.

CHARLIE

Did you smell it?

NANCY

Yes; fishy. And beautiful!

CHARLIE

Terrifying!

NANCY (*Agreeing*)

Yes; beautiful.

LESLIE

Well, I suppose I'd better go over and . . .
            (*Sort of shrugs*)

SARAH (*Immediately*)

I'll come with you.

LESLIE

No; you stay here.

SARAH (*Determined*)

I *said* I'll come *with* you.

LESLIE (*Weary*)

Yes, Sarah.

SARAH

There's no telling what kind of trouble you'll get yourself into.

LESLIE

Yes, Sarah.

SARAH

If you're going to take *that* attitude, we might as well
. . .

LESLIE (*Rather abrupt*)

All *right*, Sarah!

SARAH (*Feminine, submissive*)

All right, Leslie.

CHARLIE

What's happening?

NANCY

I think they're having a discussion.

LESLIE

Are you ready?

SARAH (*Sweet*)

Yes, dear.

LESLIE

All right?
                    (SARAH *nods*)
All right.
         (*They slowly advance toward* CHARLIE *and*
         NANCY)

CHARLIE

Here they come!

NANCY

We're making history, Charlie!

CHARLIE

(*Snorts; fear and trembling*)

The sound of one hand clapping, hunh?

> (LESLIE *and* SARAH *are before them.* LESLIE
> *raises paw to strike* CHARLIE)

SARAH

Don't hurt them.

> (LESLIE *gives* SARAH *a disapproving look, pokes*
> CHARLIE)

CHARLIE

OW!

NANCY (*Chiding*)

Charlie! Please!

CHARLIE

It poked me!

LESLIE

> (*To* CHARLIE *and* NANCY; *clears his throat*)

Pardon me.

CHARLIE (*To* NANCY)

What am I supposed to do if it pokes me?

LESLIE (*Louder*)

Pardon me.

NANCY (*Indicating* LESLIE)

Speak to it, Charlie; answer it.

CHARLIE

Hm?

NANCY

Speak to it, Charlie!

CHARLIE

"'Don't just lie there," you mean?

NANCY

I guess.
     (*Sits up and waves at* SARAH, *tentatively*)
Hello.

SARAH (*To* NANCY)

Hello.
     (*To* LESLIE)
It said hello. Did you hear it?

LESLIE

     (*His attention still on* CHARLIE)
Um-hum.

NANCY

Go on, Charlie.

SARAH

Speak to the other one.

LESLIE

I've spoken to it twice; maybe it's deaf.

NANCY

Go on.

CHARLIE

No; then I'd have to accept it.

SARAH

Maybe it's shy—or frightened. Try once again.

LESLIE (*Sighs*)

All right.
    (*Prods* CHARLIE; *says, rather too loudly and distinctly*)
Pardon me!

NANCY (*Stage whisper*)

Go *on*, Charlie.

CHARLIE

(*Pause; then, very direct*)

Hello.

(*Turns to* NANCY)

All right?

(*Back to* LESLIE)

Hello!

(*Brief silence*)

SARAH

(*Overlapping with* NANCY's *following*)
There! You see, Leslie, everything's going to be . . .

NANCY

Good for you, Charlie! Now, that wasn't so . . .
(*A raised paw and a growl from* LESLIE *silences
them both in mid-sentence*)

LESLIE

(*Moves a step toward* CHARLIE, *eyes him*)
Are you unfriendly?
(SARAH *and* NANCY *look to* CHARLIE. CHARLIE
lowers his legs and comes up on one elbow)

CHARLIE

Well . . .

NANCY

Tell him, Charlie!

CHARLIE

(*To* NANCY, *through clenched teeth*)
I'm thinking of what to say.
                    (*To* LESLIE)
Unfriendly? Well, no, not by nature. I'm certainly on my
guard, though.

LESLIE

Yes, well, so are we.

SARAH

Indeed we are!

CHARLIE

I mean, if you're going to kill us and eat us . . . then
we're unfriendly: we'll . . . resist.

LESLIE

(*Looks to* SARAH *for confirmation*)
Well, I certainly don't think we were planning to do
that. *Were* we?

SARAH (*None too sure*)

Well . . . no; at least, I don't *think* so.

NANCY

Of *course* you weren't! The very idea! Charlie, let's in-
troduce ourselves.

LESLIE

After all, you're rather large . . . and quite unusual.
(*Afterthought*)
Were you thinking of eating *us?*

NANCY (*Almost laughs*)

Good heavens, no!

SARAH

Well, we don't know your habits.

NANCY

I'm Nancy, and this is Charlie.

CHARLIE

How do. We don't know *your* habits, either. It'd be perfectly normal to assume you ate whatever . . . you ran
into . . . you know, whatever you ran into.

LESLIE (*Cool*)

No; I don't know.

SARAH (*To* NANCY)

I'm Sarah.

NANCY

Hello, Sarah.

CHARLIE

(*Somewhat on the defensive*)
It's perfectly simple: we don't eat . . . we're not canni-
bals.

LESLIE

What is this?

CHARLIE

Hm? We do eat other flesh . . . you know, cow, and
pigs, and chickens, and all . . .

LESLIE

(*To* SARAH, *very confused*)
What are *they*?

(SARAH *shrugs*)

CHARLIE

I guess you could put it down as a rule that we don't eat
anything that . . . well, anything that *talks*; you know,
English, and . . .

NANCY (*To* CHARLIE)

Parrots talk; some people eat parrots.

CHARLIE

Parrots don't *talk*; parrots *imitate*. Who eats parrots?

NANCY

In the Amazon; I'm sure people eat parrots there; they're very poor, and . . .

LESLIE

What are you *saying?!*

CHARLIE (*Frustrated*)

I'm trying to tell you . . . we don't eat our own kind.

SARAH

(*After a brief pause; flat*)

Oh.

LESLIE (*Rather offended*)

Well, we don't eat our own kind, either. Most of us. Some.

NANCY (*Cheerful*)

Well. You see?

LESLIE (*Dubious*)

Well . . .

(*To make the point*)

You see . . . you're *not* our kind, so you can understand the apprehension.

NANCY

Besides, we cook everything.

SARAH

Pardon?

NANCY

We cook everything. Well, most things; *you* know . . .
no, you don't, do you?

SARAH

This is Leslie.

NANCY

(*Extending her hand*)
How do you do, Leslie?

LESLIE

(*Regards her gesture*)
What is that?

NANCY

Oh; we . . . well, we shake hands . . . flippers, uh . . .
Charlie?

CHARLIE

When we meet we . . . take each other's hands, or whatever, and we . . . touch.

SARAH (*Pleased*)

Oh, that's *nice.*

LESLIE (*Not convinced*)

What for?

SARAH (*Chiding*)

Oh, Leslie!

LESLIE

(*To* SARAH, *a bit piqued*)
I want to know what *for.*

CHARLIE

Well, it *used* to be, since most people are right-handed,
it used to be to prove nobody had a weapon, to prove
they were friendly.

LESLIE (*After a bit*)

We're ambidextrous.

CHARLIE (*Rather miffed*)

Well, that's *nice* for you. Very nice.

NANCY

And some people used to hold on to their sex parts,
didn't you tell me that, Charlie? That in olden times

people used to hold on to their sex parts when they said
hello . . . their own?

CHARLIE

I don't think I told you quite that. Each other's, maybe.

NANCY

Well, no matter.
(*To* LESLIE)
Let's greet each other properly, all right?
(*Extends her hand again*)
I give you my hand, and you give me your . . . what *is*
that? What is that called?

LESLIE

What?

NANCY

(*Indicating* LESLIE's *right arm*)
That there.

LESLIE

It's called a leg, of course.

NANCY

Oh. Well, we call this an arm.

LESLIE

You have four arms, I see.

CHARLIE

No; she has two arms.

(*Tiny pause*)

And two legs.

SARAH

(*Moves closer to examine* NANCY *with* LESLIE)
And which are the legs?

NANCY

These here. And these are the arms.

LESLIE

(*A little on his guard*)
Why do you differentiate?

NANCY

Why do we differentiate, Charlie?

CHARLIE (*Quietly hysterical*)

Because they're the ones with the hands on the ends of
them.

NANCY (*To* LESLIE)

Yes.

SARAH

(*As* LESLIE *glances suspiciously at* CHARLIE)

Go on, Leslie; do what Nancy wants you to.
                    (*To* NANCY)
What is it called?

NANCY

Shaking hands.

CHARLIE

Or legs.

LESLIE
            (*Glowers at* CHARLIE)
Quiet.

CHARLIE (*Quickly*)

Yes, sir.

LESLIE (*To* NANCY)

Now; what is it you want to do?

NANCY

Well . . .
        (A *glance at* CHARLIE, *both reassuring and im-
        ploring*)
. . . you give me your . . . that leg there, that one, and
I'll give you my . . . leg, or arm, or whatever, and we'll
come together by our fingers . . . these are your fingers
. . .

LESLIE

Toes.

NANCY

Oh, all right; toes.
(*Shakes hands with* LESLIE)
And we come together like this, and we do this.
(*They continue a slow, broad handshake*)

LESLIE

Yes?

NANCY

And now we let go.
(*They do*)
There! You see?

LESLIE

(*Somewhat puzzled about it*)
Well, that's certainly an unusual thing to want to do.

SARAH

Let *me!* I want to!
(SARAH *shakes hands with* NANCY, *seems happy about doing it*)
Oh, my; that's very interesting.
(*To* LESLIE)
Why haven't *we* ever done anything like that?

LESLIE (*Shrugs*)

Damned if *I* know.

SARAH

(*To* LESLIE, *referring to* CHARLIE)
You do it with *him*, now.
(CHARLIE *smiles tentatively, holds his hand out
a little;* LESLIE *moves over to him*)

LESLIE

Are you *sure* you're friendly?

CHARLIE

(*Nervous, but serious*)
I *told* you: you'll never meet a more peaceful man.
Though of course if I thought you were going to go at
me, or Nancy here, I'd probably defend myself . . . I
mean, I *would*.

LESLIE

The danger, as *I* see it, is if one of us panics.
(CHARLIE *gives a hollow laugh*)
I think I'd like to know what frightens you.
(CHARLIE *laughs again*)

Please?

NANCY (*Nicely*)

Tell him, Charlie.

SARAH

Please?

CHARLIE

(A *pause, while the nature of his questioner sinks in*)
What frightens me? Oh . . . deep space? Mortality?
Nancy . . . not being with me?
                    (*Chuckles ruefully*)
Great . . . green . . . creatures coming up from the sea.

LESLIE

Well, that's it, you see: what we don't *know*. Great
green creatures, and all, indeed! You're pretty odd your-
selves, though you've probably never looked at it that
way.

CHARLIE

Probably not.

LESLIE

You're not the sort of thing we run into every day.

CHARLIE

Well, *no* . . .

LESLIE (*Points at* CHARLIE)

What's all *that?*

CHARLIE (*Looks at himself*)

What?

LESLIE

(*Touches* CHARLIE's *shirt; says it with some distaste*)
All *that*.

CHARLIE

This? My shirt.
(*"Naturally" implicit*)

LESLIE

What *is* it?

NANCY

Clothes; they're called clothes; we put them on; we . . .
well, we cover our skins with them.

LESLIE

What for?

NANCY

Well . . . to keep warm; to look pretty; to be decent.

LESLIE

What is *that*?

NANCY

Which?

LESLIE

Decent.

NANCY

Oh. Well . . . uh, not to expose our sexual parts. My breasts, for example.
                    (*Touches them*)

CHARLIE

Say "mammaries."

NANCY

What?

SARAH (*Fascinated*)

What *are* they?

NANCY

Well, they . . . no, you don't seem to have them, do you? They're . . . secondary sex organs.
            (*Realizes it's hopeless as she says it*)
No? well . . .
      (*Beckons* SARAH, *begins to unbutton her blouse*)
Come here, Sarah.

CHARLIE

Nancy!

NANCY

It's all *right*, Charlie. Come look, Sarah.

SARAH

(*Puts one paw on* NANCY's *blouse, peers in*)
My gracious! Leslie, come see!

CHARLIE

Now just a minute!

NANCY (*Laughs*)

Charlie! Don't be silly!

LESLIE

(*To* CHARLIE; *ingenuous*)
What's the matter?

CHARLIE

I don't want you looking at my wife's breasts, that's all.

LESLIE

I don't even know what they are.

NANCY (*Buoyant*)

Of course not! Are you *jealous*, Charlie?

CHARLIE

Of course not! How could I be jealous of . . .
        (*Indicates* LESLIE *with some distaste*)
. . . how *could* I be?

NANCY (*Agreeing with him*)

No.

CHARLIE (*Reassuring himself*)

I'm *not*.

SARAH (*No overtones*)

I think Leslie *should* see them.

NANCY

Yes.

LESLIE

(*To* CHARLIE; *shrugs*)

It's up to *you*; I mean, if they're something you *hide*,
then maybe they're embarrassing, or sad, and I shouldn't
want to see them, and . . .

CHARLIE

(*More flustered than angry*)
They're not embarrassing; *or* sad; They're lovely! Some
women . . . some women Nancy's age, they're . . . some
women . . .
(*To* NANCY, *almost spontaneously bursting into tears*)
I *love* your breasts.

NANCY (*Gentle*)

Yes; *yes. Thank* you.
(*More expansive*)
I'm not an exhibitionist, dear, as you very well know . . .

CHARLIE

. . . except that time you answered the door stark
naked . . .

NANCY (*An old story*)

We'll not discuss that now.
(*To* LESLIE *and* SARAH)
It was nothing.

CHARLIE (*By rote*)

So *she* says.

NANCY (*To the others*)

It was nothing. Really.

(*To* CHARLIE)

What I was trying to say, Charlie, was—and prefacing it
with that I'm not an exhibitionist, as you very well know
—that if someone . . .

CHARLIE (*To* NANCY)

Stark naked.

NANCY

. . . has *not* . . . has gone through life and *not* seen a
woman's breasts . . . why, it's like Sarah never having
seen . . . the sky. Think of the wonder of *that*, and
think of the wonder of the other.

CHARLIE (*Rather hurt*)

One of the wonders, hunh?

NANCY

I didn't *mean* it that way!
          (*Shakes her head; buttons up*)
Well . . . no matter.

LESLIE (*Shrugs*)

It's up to you.

SARAH

They're really very interesting, Leslie; I'm sorry you
didn't see them.

LESLIE

Well, another time, maybe.

SARAH

(*Delighted and excited*)

I suddenly remember something! Leslie, do you remember when we went way north, and it was very cold,
and the scenery changed, and we came to the edge of a
deep ravine, and all at once we heard those strange and
terrible sounds . . .

LESLIE

(*Disturbed at the memory*)

Yes; I remember.

SARAH

Oh, it was a frightening set of sounds, echoing . . . all
around us; and then we saw them . . . swimming by.

LESLIE

Enormous . . .

SARAH

Huge! Huge creatures; ten of them, maybe more. I'd
never seen the size. They were of great girth.

CHARLIE

They were whales; I'm sure they were whales.

LESLIE

Is *that* what they were?

SARAH

We observed them, though, and they had young with them; young! And it was most interesting: the young would attach themselves to what I assume was the female—the mother—would attach themselves to devices that I *think* were very much like those of *yours*; resemble them.

NANCY

Of course! To the mammaries! Oh, Sarah, those *were* whales, for whales are mammals and they feed their young.

SARAH

Do you remember, Leslie?

LESLIE (*Nods*)

Yes, I think I do.
(*To* NANCY)
And you have those? That's what *you* have?

NANCY

Yes; well . . . very much like them . . . in principle.

LESLIE

My gracious.

CHARLIE

(*To clear the air; brisk*)
Do you, uh . . . do *you* have any children? Any young?

SARAH (*Laughs gaily*)

Well, of course I have! Hundreds!

CHARLIE

Hundreds!

SARAH

Certainly; I'm laying eggs all the time.

CHARLIE (*A pause*)

You . . . lay eggs.

SARAH

Certainly! Right and left.
(*A pause*)

NANCY

Well.

LESLIE (*Eyes narrowed*)

You, uh . . . you *don't* lay eggs, hunh?

CHARLIE (*Incredulous*)

No; of course not!

LESLIE (*Exploding*)

There! You see?! What did I tell you?! They don't even
lay eggs!

NANCY

(*Trying to save the situation*)
How many . . . uh . . . eggs have you laid, Sarah?

SARAH
(*Thinks about it for a bit*)
Seven thousand?

NANCY (*Admonishing*)

Oh! Sarah!

SARAH

No?

NANCY

Well, I dare say! Yes! But, really!

SARAH

I'm sorry?

NANCY

No! Never that!

CHARLIE

(*To* LESLIE, *with some awe*)
Seven thousand! Really?

LESLIE

(*Gruff; the usual husband*)
Well, *I* don't know. I mean . . .

NANCY

What do you *do* with them, Sarah? How do you take
care of them?

SARAH

Well . . . they just . . . float away.

NANCY (*Chiding*)

Oh, Sarah!

SARAH

Some get eaten—by folk passing by, which is a blessing,
really, or we'd be inundated—some fall to the bottom,
some catch on growing things; there's a disposition.

NANCY

Still!

SARAH

Why? What do *you* do with them?

NANCY

(*Looks at her nails briefly*)
It's different with us, Sarah. In the birthing, I mean; I don't know about . . . well, how you go about it!

SARAH (*Shy*)

Well . . . we couple.

LESLIE

Shhh!

NANCY

Yes; I thought. And so do we.

SARAH (*Relieved*)

Oh; good. And then—in a few weeks—

NANCY

Oh, it takes a lot longer for us, Sarah: nine months.

SARAH

Nine months! Leslie!

LESLIE

Wow!

SARAH

Nine months.

NANCY

And then the young are born. *Is* born . . . usually.

SARAH

Hm?

NANCY

Is. We usually have one, Sarah. One at a time. Oh, two, occasionally; rarely three or more.

SARAH (*Commiserating*)

Oh, Nancy!

LESLIE (*To* CHARLIE)

If you have only one or two, what if they're washed away, or eaten? I mean, how do you . . . perpetuate?

NANCY (*Gay laugh*)

That never happens. We keep them with us . . . till they're all grown up and ready for the world.

SARAH

How long is that?

CHARLIE

Eighteen . . . twenty years.

LESLIE

You're not serious!

NANCY

Oh, we *are!*

LESLIE

You *can't* be.

CHARLIE (*Defensive*)

Why not?!

LESLIE

Well . . . I mean . . . *think* about it.

CHARLIE (*Does*)

Well . . . it *is* a long time, I suppose, but there's no other way for it.

NANCY

Just as you let them float away, or get caught on things; there's no other way for it.

SARAH

How many have you birthed?

NANCY

Three.

SARAH

(*Still with the wonder of that*)
Only three.

NANCY

Of course, there's *another* reason we keep them with us.

SARAH

Oh? What is that?

NANCY

(*Puzzled at her question*)
Well . . . we *love* them.
(*Pause*)

LESLIE

Pardon?

CHARLIE

We *love* them.

LESLIE

Explain.

CHARLIE

What?

LESLIE

What you said.

CHARLIE

We said we love them.

LESLIE

Yes; explain.

CHARLIE (*Incredulous*)

What love means?!

NANCY (*To* SARAH)

Love? Love is one of the emotions.

(*They look at her, waiting*)
One of the *emotions*, Sarah.

SARAH

(*After a tiny pause*)
But, what *are* they?!

NANCY (*Becoming impatient*)

Well, you *must* have them. You *must* have *emotions*.

LESLIE (*Quite impatient*)

We may, or we may not, but we'll never know unless
you define your terms. Honestly, the imprecision! You're
so thoughtless!

CHARLIE (*Miffed*)

Well, we're sorry!

LESLIE

You have to make allowances!

CHARLIE

All *right!!*

LESLIE

Just . . . thoughtless.

CHARLIE

All *right!*

SARAH

Help us, Nancy.

NANCY
(*To* SARAH *and* LESLIE)

Fear. Hatred. Apprehension. Loss. Love.
(*Pause*)
Nothing?
(*A bedtime story*)
We keep them with us because they need us to; and we
feel possessive toward them, and grateful, and proud . . .

CHARLIE (*Ironic*)

And lots of *other* words describing emotions. You can't
do that, Nancy; it doesn't help.

NANCY (*Annoyed*)

Then *you* do it! And when we get back home, I'm packing up and taking a good long trip. *Alone.* I've been
married to you far too smoothly for far too long.

CHARLIE (*To* LESLIE)

That's an example of emotion: frustration, anger . . .

NANCY (*To herself*)

I'm too *old* to have an affair.
(*Pause*)
No, I'm not.

(*Pause*)

Yes, I am.

CHARLIE (*Chuckling*)

Oh, come on, Nancy.

(*To* LESLIE *and* SARAH)

Maybe *I* can do it. How did you two get together?
How'd ya meet?

LESLIE

Well, I was just going along, one day, minding my own
business . . .

SARAH

Oh, Leslie!

(*To* CHARLIE)

I was reaching my maturity, and so, naturally, a lot of
males were paying attention to me—milling around—you
know, preening and snapping at each other and generally
showing off, and I noticed one was hanging around a little distance away, not joining in with the others . . .

LESLIE

That was me.

SARAH

. . . and I didn't pay too much attention to him, because I thought he was probably sickly or something,
and besides, there were so many others, and it was time
to start coupling . . .

LESLIE

You noticed me.

SARAH

. . . when, all of a sudden! There he was, right in the middle of them, snapping away, really fighting, driving all the others off. It was quite a rumpus.

LESLIE

(*An aside, to* CHARLIE)
They didn't *amount* to much.

SARAH (*Shrugs*)

And so . . . all the others drifted away . . . and there he was.

LESLIE

They didn't *drift* away: I drove them away.

SARAH

Well, I suppose that's true.
(*Bright*)
Show them your scar, Leslie!
(*To* CHARLIE *and* NANCY)
Leslie has a marvelous scar!

LESLIE (*Proud*)

Oh . . . some other time.

SARAH

And there he *was* . . . and there *I* was . . . and here we *are*.

CHARLIE

Well, yes! That proves my point!

LESLIE

What?

CHARLIE

(*Pause*)

About *love*.

(*Pause*)

He *loved* you.

SARAH

Yes?

CHARLIE

Well, *yes*. He drove the others away so he could have *you*. He wanted *you*.

SARAH

(*As if what* CHARLIE *has said proves nothing*)

Ye-es?

CHARLIE

Well . . . it's so *clear*. Nancy, isn't it clear?

NANCY

I don't *know*. Don't talk to me; you're a terrible person.

CHARLIE (*Under his breath*)

Oh, for God's sake! Leslie! *Why* did you want Sarah?

LESLIE

Well, as I told you: I was just going along one day, minding my own business, and there was this great commotion, with all the others around her, and so I decided *I* wanted her.

CHARLIE (*Losing, but game*)

Didn't you think she was . . . pretty—or whatever?

LESLIE

I couldn't really see, with all the others hovering. She *smelled* all right.

CHARLIE

Have you ever, you know, coupled with anyone else since you met Sarah?

NANCY

Charlie!

LESLIE

(*Pause; too defensive*)
Why should I?

CHARLIE (*Smiles*)

Just asking.
(*Patient*)
Is that your *nature*? Not to go around coupling when-
ever you feel like it, whatever female strikes your fancy?

SARAH (*Fascinated*)

V*ery* interesting.

LESLIE (*To shut her up*)

It is *not!*
(*To* CHARLIE)
I've coupled in my time.

CHARLIE

Since you met Sarah?

LESLIE

I'm not going to *answer* that.

SARAH (*Hurt*)

You *have?*

CHARLIE

No; he means he hasn't. And he's embarrassed by it.
What about you, Sarah? Have you been with anyone
since Leslie?

LESLIE

Of *course* she hasn't!

NANCY

What an *awful* question to ask Sarah! You should be
ashamed of yourself!

CHARLIE

It's not an awful question at all.

NANCY

It *is!* It's dreadful! Of course she hasn't.

CHARLIE (*Annoyed*)

What *standards* are you using? How would *you* know?

NANCY

(*Up on her high horse*)

I just know.

CHARLIE

Things might be different, you know . . .
                    (*Gestures vaguely around*)
. . . down . . . *there*. I don't think it's dreadful at *all*.

SARAH

(*To* NANCY *and* CHARLIE)
The truth of the matter is: no, I haven't.

LESLIE

What are you getting at?!

CHARLIE

It's hard to explain!

LESLIE

Apparently.

CHARLIE

Especially to someone who has no grasp of conceptual
matters, who hasn't heard of half the words in the English language, who lives on the bottom of the sea and
has green scales!

LESLIE

Look, buddy . . . !

| SARAH | NANCY |
Leslie . . .   Now you two boys just. . .

CHARLIE (*Half to himself*)

Might as well be talking to a fish.

LESLIE

(*Really angry; starts toward* CHARLIE)
That does it!

NANCY

Charlie! Look out! Sarah, stop him!

SARAH (*Stamps her paw*)

Leslie! You be nice!

LESLIE (*To* SARAH)

He called me a fish!

SARAH

He did not!

NANCY

No he didn't; not quite. He said he might as well.

LESLIE

Same thing.

CHARLIE

(*A glint in his eye*)
Oh? What's the matter with fish?

NANCY (*Sotto voce*)

Calm down, Charlie . . .

CHARLIE (*Persisting*)

What's the matter with fish, hunh?

SARAH

Be good, Leslie . . .

LESLIE

(*On his high horse—so to speak*)
We just don't think very highly of fish, that's all.

CHARLIE

(*Seeing a triumph somewhere*)
Oh? You don't like fish, hunh?

NANCY

Now, *both* of you!

CHARLIE

What's the matter with fish all of a sudden?

LESLIE

(*Real middle class, but not awful*)
For one thing, there're too many of them; they're all
over the place . . . racing around, darting in front of
you, *picking* at everything . . . moving in, taking over
where you live . . . and they're stupid!

SARAH (*Shy*)

Not all of them; porpoises aren't stupid.

LESLIE (*Still wound up*)

All right! Except for porpoises . . . they're stupid!
          (*Thinks about it some more*)
And they're dirty!

CHARLIE

(*Mouth opens in amazement and delight*)
You're . . . you're prejudiced! Nancy, he's . . . You're a
bigot!
          (*Laughs*)
You're a goddamn bigot!

LESLIE (*Dangerous*)

Yeah? What's that?

NANCY

Be careful, Charlie.

LESLIE (*Not amused*)

What *is* that?

CHARLIE

What? A bigot?

LESLIE

I don't know. Is that what you said?

CHARLIE (*Right on with it*)

A bigot is somebody who thinks he's better than somebody else because they're different.

LESLIE

(*Brief pause; anger defused*)
Oh; well, then; that's all right. I'm not what you said. It's *not* because they're different: it's because they're stupid and they're dirty and they're all over the place!

CHARLIE

(*Parody of studying and accepting*)
Oh. Well. That's all right, then.

NANCY (*Wincing some*)

Careful, Charlie.

LESLIE

(*Absorbed with his own words*)
Being different is . . . interesting; there's nothing implicitly inferior or superior about it. *Great* difference, of course, produces natural caution; and if the differences are too extreme . . . well, then, reality tends to fade away.

NANCY

(*An aside; to* CHARLIE)
And so much for conceptual matters.

CHARLIE

(*Dismissing it with bravado*)
Oooooooh, he probably read it somewhere.

SARAH

(*Looks at the sky, and about her, expansively*)
My! It *is* quite something out here, isn't it? You can see! So very far!
(*She sees birds with some consternation*)
What are those?
(LESLIE *sees them. Tenses. Does an intake of breath*)

NANCY

(looking up)

Birds. Those are birds, Sarah.

(LESLIE *in reaction to the birds starts moving
up the dune*)

SARAH

Leslie! Leslie!

(LESLIE *continues to move to top of the dune;
growling*)

NANCY

What's he doing?

SARAH

He's . . .

(*Shrugs*)

. . . well, he does it everywhere we go, so why not up
here? He checks things out, makes sure a way is open for
us . . .

CHARLIE

It's called instinct.

SARAH

(*Polite, but not terribly interested*)

Oh? *Is* it.

CHARLIE (*Nods; quite happy*)

Instinct.

SARAH

Well, this isn't the sort of situation we run into every day, *and* . . . creatures do tend to be devious; you don't know what's going to happen from one minute to the next . . .

NANCY

Certainly, certainly. Will he be all right? I mean . . .

SARAH

Oh, certainly. He's kind and he's a good mate, and when he tells me what we're going to do, I find I can live with it quite nicely. And you?

NANCY

Uh . . . well, we manage rather like that I guess.

SARAH (*Rapt*)

Oh, my goodness; *see* them up there! How they *go!*

CHARLIE

Seagulls.

SARAH

Sea . . . gulls.
                (*Still absorbed*)
The wonder of it! What holds them up?

CHARLIE (*Shy, but helpful*)

Aerodynamics.

SARAH (*Still enraptured*)

Indeed.

NANCY

Tsk.

CHARLIE (*Feelings hurt*)

Well, it *is*.

SARAH (*To him*)

Oh, I wasn't *doubting* it.
                (*Attention back to the birds*)
See them swim!

CHARLIE

                (*More sure of himself now*)
Fly, they fly; birds fly.

SARAH (*Watching the birds*)

The rays are rather like that: swimming about; what do
you call it—flying. Funny creatures; shy, really; don't give
that impression, though; stand-offish, rather curt.

NANCY

Rays. Yes; well, we know them.

SARAH (*Pleased*)

Do you!

CHARLIE

Nancy means we've *seen* them; photographs.

SARAH

What is *that?*

CHARLIE

Photographs? It's a . . . no, I'd better not try.

SARAH (*Coquettish*)

Something I shouldn't know? Something you could tell
Leslie but not me?

NANCY (*Laughs*)

Heavens, no!

SARAH

I mean, I *am* a married woman.

CHARLIE (*Surprised*)

Do you *do* that? I mean, do you . . . ? I don't know
what I mean.

NANCY

Charlie! Just think what we can tell our children and our
grandchildren: that we were here when Sarah saw it all!

CHARLIE

Sure! And if you think they'd have us put away for all
that other—for living on the beach . . .

NANCY (*Nodding along*)

. . . "from beach to beach, seaside nomads . . ."

CHARLIE

. . . yes, then *what* do you *think* they'd *say* about *this!*
(*Mimics her*)
"Charlie and I were sitting around, you see, when all at
once, lo and behold, these two great green lizards . . ."
How do you think they'd take to *that?!* Put it in one of
your postcards, Nancy, and mail it out.

NANCY

Ohhhhh, Charlie! You give me the pip, you know that?

SARAH

(*Calling to* LESLIE)

Leslie, Leslie.

LESLIE

(LESLIE *cautiously starts down the dune*)

Are you all right?

SARAH

Oh, Leslie, I've had an absolutely fascinating time. Leslie . . .

(*Points to the sky*)

. . . up there.

LESLIE

What *are* they?

SARAH (*Bubbling with it*)

They're called *birds*, and they don't swim, they fly, and
they stay up by something called aerodynamics . . .

LESLIE

What is *that?*

SARAH (*Rushing on*)

I'm sure I don't know, and *I* said they looked like rays,
and *they* said they knew rays through something called

photographs, though they wouldn't tell me what that *was*, and Charlie gives Nancy the pip.

LESLIE

There, I was right! You can't trust somebody like that! How can you trust somebody like that? You can't trust somebody like that!

NANCY

(*With a desperate attempt to save the situation*)
Well, what does it matter? We're all *dead.*

SARAH

Dead? Who's dead?

NANCY

We are.

SARAH (*Disbelief*)

No.

NANCY

According to Charlie here.

CHARLIE (*Without humor*)

It's not to be joked about.

SARAH

All of us?

NANCY (*Chuckles*)

Well, I'm not certain about that; he and I, apparently.
It all has to do with liver paste. The fatal sandwich.

CHARLIE

Explain it right! Leave it alone if you're not going to give
it the dignity it deserves.

NANCY

(*To* LESLIE *and* SARAH; *a trifle patronizing*)
I mean, we *have* to be dead, because Charlie has decided
that the wonders do not occur; that what we have not
known does not exist; that what we cannot fathom cannot be; that the miracles, if you will, are bedtime stories;
he has taken the leap of faith, from agnostic to atheist;
the world is flat; the sun and the planets revolve about it,
and don't row out too far or you'll fall off.

CHARLIE (*Sad; embarrassed*)

I couldn't live with you again; I'm glad it doesn't matter.

NANCY (*To* CHARLIE; *nicely*)

Oh, Charlie.

LESLIE

(*To* CHARLIE, *not believing any of it*)
When did you die?

CHARLIE

Pardon?

SARAH

(*To* NANCY; *whispering*)
He's not dead.

NANCY (*To* SARAH)

I know.

LESLIE

Did we frighten you to death, or was it before we met
you?

CHARLIE

Oh, *before* we met you; after lunch.

LESLIE

Then I take it *we* don't *exist*.

CHARLIE (*Apologetic*)

Probably not; I'm sorry.

LESLIE (*To* NANCY)

That's quite a mind he's got there.

NANCY

(*Grudgingly defending* CHARLIE)
Well . . . he thinks things through.
(*Very cheerful*)
As for *me*, I couldn't care less: I'm having far too interesting a time.

SARAH

Oh, I'm so glad!

LESLIE (*Puzzled*)

I *think* I exist.

CHARLIE (*Shrugs*)

Well, *that's* all that matters; it's the same thing.

NANCY

(*To* SARAH; *considerable enthusiasm*)
Oh, a voice from the dead.

LESLIE (*To* CHARLIE)

You mean it's all an illusion?

CHARLIE

Could be.

LESLIE

The whole thing? Existence?

CHARLIE

Um-hum!

LESLIE

(*Sitting down with* CHARLIE)
I don't believe *that* at *all*.

CHARLIE

Well, it isn't *my* theory.

LESLIE

Whose theory *is* it, then?

CHARLIE (*Angry*)

What?!

LESLIE

Whose theory *is* it? Don't you yell at me.

CHARLIE

I am not *yelling* at you!

LESLIE

Yes, you are! You *did!*

CHARLIE

Well, then, I'm sorry.

LESLIE

Whose *theory* is it?

CHARLIE (*Weary*)

Descartes.

LESLIE (*Annoyed*)

What is *that?*

CHARLIE

What?

LESLIE

What you *said.*

CHARLIE (*Barely in control*)

DESCARTES!! DESCARTES!! I THINK: THERE-
FORE I AM!!
(*Pause*)
COGITO! ERGO! SUM! I THINK: THEREFORE I
AM!!

(*Pause. Pleading*)
Now you're going to ask me what *think* means.

NANCY

(*Comforting, moving to him, genuine*)
No, he's *not*; he wouldn't *do* that.

CHARLIE

I haven't got it *in* me.

NANCY

It's all right.

LESLIE (*To* SARAH)

I know what think means.

SARAH

Of course you do!

LESLIE (*Agreeing*)

Well!

CHARLIE

I couldn't take it.

NANCY

It's not going to happen.

CHARLIE

It's more than I could . . . Death is release, if you've
lived all right, and *I* have.
        (NANCY *hugs him, but he goes on*)
As well as most, easily; when it comes time, and I put
down my fork on the plate, line it up with the knife,
take a last sip of wine, or water, touch my lips and fold
the napkin, push back the chair . . .

NANCY

    (*Shakes him by the shoulders, looks him in the
    eye*)
Charlie!
    (*Kisses him on the mouth, her tongue enter-
    ing, for quite a little; he is passive, then slowly
    responds, taking comfort, and sharing; they
    come apart, finally; he shrugs, chuckles timidly,
    smiles, chucks her under the chin*)

CHARLIE (*Shy*)

Well.

NANCY

It is all *right*; and you're alive. It's all right and, if it isn't
. . . well, it will just have to do. No matter what.

CHARLIE (*Irony*)

This will have to do.

NANCY

Yes, this will have to do.

SARAH

Is he all right?

NANCY

Well . . . he's been through life, you see and . . . yes, I
suppose he's all right.
> (*The sound of the jet plane again from stage
> left to stage right, growing, becoming deafen-
> ingly loud, diminishing.*
> CHARLIE *and* NANCY *follow its course;* LESLIE
> *and* SARAH *are terrified; they rush half out of
> sight over the dune*)

NANCY

> (*In the silence following the plane*)
Such *noise* they make.

CHARLIE

They'll crash into the dunes one day; I don't know what
good they do.

NANCY

> (*Seeing* LESLIE *and* SARAH, *pointing to them*)
Oh, Charlie! Look! Look at them!

CHARLIE

Hm? What?

(*Sees them*)

Oh!

NANCY

Oh, Charlie; they're frightened. They're so frightened!

CHARLIE (*Awe*)

They are.

LESLIE

(*From where he is; calling*)

What *was* that?!

NANCY

(*Calling; a light tone*)

It was an aeroplane.

LESLIE

Well, what *is* it?!

CHARLIE

It's a machine that . . . it's a method of . . .

LESLIE

What?

CHARLIE (*Shouting*)

It's a machine that . . . it's a method of . . .
> (LESLIE *and* SARAH *begin to move back, paw in*
> *paw, glancing back at the plane as they move*)
It's a . . . it's like a bird, except that we make them—we
put them together, and we get inside them, and that's
how we fly . . . sort of.

SARAH (*Some awe*)

It's terrifying!

NANCY

Well, you get used to it.

LESLIE

> (*To* CHARLIE; *to get it straight*)
You . . . fly.

CHARLIE

Yes. Well, some do. *I* have. Yes! *I* fly. We do all sorts of
things up here.

LESLIE

I'll bet you do.

CHARLIE

Sure; give us a machine and there isn't anywhere we

won't go. Why, we even have a machine that will . . .
go down there; under water.

LESLIE (*Brow furrowed*)

Then . . . you've *been*—what do you call it: under
water?

CHARLIE

Well, not in one of the machines, no. And nowhere near
as deep as . . .

NANCY

Charlie *used* to go under—near the shore, of course; not
very deep.

CHARLIE

Oh, God . . . years ago.

NANCY

Yes, and Charlie has missed it. He was telling me how
much he used to love to go down under, settle on the
bottom, wait for the fish to come . . .

CHARLIE

(*Embarrassed; indicating* LESLIE *and* SARAH)
It was a *long* time ago.
(*To* NANCY)
Nancy, not now! Please!

LESLIE (*Very interested*)

Really.

CHARLIE

It didn't *amount* to much.

NANCY

Oh, it *did*; it *did* amount, and to a great deal.

CHARLIE

(*Embarrassed and angry*)
Lay off, Nancy!

NANCY

(*Turns on* CHARLIE, *impatient and angry*)
It used to make you *happy*, and you used to be *proud* of
what made you happy!

CHARLIE

LEAVE OFF!!
(*Subsides*)
Just . . . leave off.
(*A silence. Now, to* LESLIE *and* SARAH; *quietly*)
It was just a game; it was enough for a twelve-year-old,
maybe, but it wasn't . . . finding out, you know; it
wasn't *real*. It wasn't enough for a memory.
(*Pause; shakes his head*)

CHARLIE

(*Barely controlled rage; to* LESLIE)
Why did you come up here in the first place?

LESLIE (*Too matter-of-fact*)

I don't know.

CHARLIE (*Thunder*)

COME! ON!

LESLIE

I don't know!
(*To* SARAH; *too offhand*)
Do I know?

SARAH (*Yes and no*)

Well . . .

LESLIE (*Final*)

I don't know.

SARAH

We had a sense of not belonging any more.

LESLIE

Don't, Sarah.

SARAH

I should, Leslie. It was a growing thing, nothing abrupt,
nor that anything was different, for that matter.

LESLIE (*Helpless*)

Don't go on, Sarah.

SARAH

. . . in the sense of having changed; but . . . *we* had
changed . . .
           (*Looks about her*)
. . . all of a sudden, everything . . . down there . . . was
terribly . . . interesting, I suppose; but what did it have
to do with *us* any more?

LESLIE

Don't, Sarah.

SARAH

And it wasn't . . . comfortable any more. I mean, after
all, you make your nest, and accept a whole . . . array
. . . of things . . . and . . . we didn't feel we *belonged*
there any more. And . . . what were we going to do?!

CHARLIE

           (*After a little; shy*)
And that's why you came up.

LESLIE (*Nods, glumly*)

We talked about it.

SARAH

Yes. We did, for a long time. Considered the pros and
the cons. Making do down there or trying something
else. But what?

CHARLIE

And so you came up.

LESLIE

Is that what we did? Is that what we were doing? I don't
know.

CHARLIE

(*He has hardly been listening; speaks to himself more than to anyone else*)
All that time; the eons.

LESLIE

Hm?

NANCY

What was that, Charlie?

CHARLIE

The eons. How long is an eon?

NANCY (*Encouraging him*)

A very long time.

CHARLIE

A hundred million years? Ten times that? Well, a distance certainly. What do they call it . . . the primordial soup? the glop? That heartbreaking second when it all got together, the sugars and the acids and the ultraviolets, and the next thing you knew there were tangerines and string quartets.

LESLIE

What are *they?*

CHARLIE

(*Smiles, a little sadly, shrugs*)

It doesn't matter. But somewhere in all that time, halfway, probably, halfway between the aminos and the treble clef—

(*Directed to* SARAH *and* LESLIE)

listen to this—there was a time when we *all* were down there, crawling around, and swimming and carrying on— remember how we read about it, Nancy . . .

NANCY

Yes . . . crawling around, and swimming . . . rather like
it is now, but very different.

CHARLIE

Yes; very.
                    (*To* LESLIE *and* SARAH)
Are you interested in any of this?

SARAH (*Genuine, and pert*)

Oh! Fascinated!

CHARLIE

And you understand it; I mean, you follow it.

LESLIE

                    (*Hurt, if not quite sure of himself*)
Of *course* we follow it.

SARAH (*Wavering a little*)

Of . . . of course.

NANCY

Of *course* they do.

LESLIE (*A kind of bluff*)

"Rather like it is now, but very different" . . .
                    (*Shrugs*)
Whatever that means.

CHARLIE

                    (*Enthusiastic didacticism*)
It means that once upon a time you and I lived down
there.

LESLIE

Oh, come on!

CHARLIE

Well, no, not literally, and *not* you and me, for that
matter, but what we became.

LESLIE

                    (*Feigning enthusiastic belief*)
Um-hum; um-hum.

SARAH

When were we all down there?

CHARLIE

Oh, a long time ago.

NANCY

Once upon a time, Sarah.

SARAH (*After a pause*)

Yes?

NANCY

(*Laughs, realizing she is supposed to continue*)
Oh my goodness. I feel silly.

CHARLIE

Why? All you're going to do is explain evolution to a couple of lizards.

NANCY (*Rising above it*)

Once upon a time, Sarah, a long, long time ago, long before you were born—even before Charlie here was born . . .

CHARLIE

(*Feigning great boredom*)
Veeeerrry funny.

NANCY

Nothing was like it is at all today. There were fish, but they didn't look like any fish you've ever seen.

SARAH

My goodness!

LESLIE

What happened to them?

NANCY

(*Trying to find it exactly*)
Well . . . they were dissatisfied, is what they were. So, they grew, or diminished, or . . . or sprouted things— tails, spots, fins, feathers.

SARAH

It sounds extremely busy.

NANCY

Well, it *was*. Of course, it didn't happen all at once.

SARAH (*Looks to* LESLIE)

Oh?

NANCY (*A pleased laugh*)

Oh, *heavens* no. Small changes; adding up. Like . . . well, there probably was a time when Leslie didn't have a tail.

SARAH (*Laughs*)

Oh, really!

LESLIE (*Quite dry*)

I've always had a tail.

NANCY (*Bright*)

Oh, no; there was a time, way back, you didn't. Before
you needed it you didn't have one.

LESLIE (*Through his teeth*)

I have *always* had a *tail*.

SARAH

Leslie's very proud of his tail, Nancy . . .

CHARLIE

You like your tail, do you?

LESLIE

(*Grim; gathers his tail in front of him*)
I have *always* had a *tail*.

SARAH

Of course you have, Leslie; it's a lovely tail.

LESLIE

Hugging his tail in front of him, anxiety on his face)
I have. I've always had one.

NANCY (*Trying again*)

Well, of course you have, and so did your father before you, and his, too, I have no doubt, and so on back, but maybe they had a smaller tail than you, or a larger.

LESLIE

Smaller!

SARAH

Leslie's extremely proud of his tail; it's very large and sturdy and . . .

NANCY

Well, I'm sure; yes.

LESLIE (*Eyeing* CHARLIE)

You don't have a tail.

CHARLIE (*Rather proud*)

No, I don't.

LESLIE

What happened to it?

CHARLIE

It fell off. Mutate or perish. Let your tail drop off, change your spots, or maybe just your point of view. The dinosaurs knew a thing or two, but that was about it . . . great, enormous creatures, big as a diesel engine—
(*To* LESLIE)
whatever that may be—leviathans! . . . with a brain the size of a lichee nut; couldn't cope; couldn't figure it all out; went down.

LESLIE (*Quite disgusted*)

What are you talking about?

CHARLIE

Just running on, and trying to make a point. And do you know what happened once? Kind of the crowning moment of it all for me? It was when some . . . slimy creature poked his head out of the muck, looked around, and decided to spend some time up here . . . Came up into the air and decided to stay? And as time went on, he split apart and evolved and became tigers and gazelles and porcupines and Nancy here . . .

LESLIE (*Annoyed*)

I don't believe a word of this!

CHARLIE

Oh, you'd better, for he went back under, too; part of
what he became didn't fancy it up on land, and went
back down there, and turned into porpoises and sharks,
and manta rays, and whales . . . and you.

LESLIE

Come off it!

CHARLIE

It's called flux. And it's always going on; right now, to all
of us.

SARAH (*Shy*)

Is it . . . is it for the better?

CHARLIE

Is it for the *better*? I don't *know*. Progress is a set of as-
sumptions. It's very beautiful down there. It's all still,
and the fish float by. It's very beautiful.

LESLIE

Don't get taken in.

CHARLIE

What are you going to tell me about? Slaughter and
pointlessness? Come on *up* here. *Stay*. The optimists say

you mustn't look just yet, that it's all going to work out
fine, no matter *what* you've heard. The pessimists, on
the other hand . . .

NANCY

It *is*. It all *is*.

CHARLIE (*Slightly mocking*)

Why?!

NANCY

Because I couldn't bear to think of it otherwise, that's
why. I'm not one of these people says that I'm better
than a . . . a rabbit; just that I'm more interesting: I use
tools, I make art . . .
          (*Turning introspective*)
. . . and I'm aware of my own mortality.
                    (*Pause*)
Very.
          (*Pouting; very much like a little girl*)
All rabbits do is eat carrots.

SARAH

          (*To* CHARLIE; *after a little pause; sotto voce*)
What are carrots?

CHARLIE

          (*Shrugs it off; not interested*)
Oh . . . something you eat. They make noise.

LESLIE (*Curiously bitter*)

And tools; and art; and mortality? Do you eat *them*?
And do *they* make a noise?

CHARLIE

(*Staring hard at* LESLIE)
They make a noise.

NANCY (*She, too*)

What is it, Leslie?

LESLIE (*Intense and angry*)

What *are* these things?!

NANCY

Tools; art; mortality?

CHARLIE

They're what separate *us* from the brute beast.

NANCY (*Very quiet*)

No, Charlie; don't.

LESLIE

(*Quiet, cold, and formal*)
You'll have to forgive me, but what is brute beast?

NANCY

Charlie; no!

CHARLIE (*Defiant*)

Brute beast?

LESLIE (*Grim*)

I don't like the sound of it.

CHARLIE (*Stares right at him*)

Brute beast? It's not even aware it's *alive*, much less that it's going to die!

LESLIE

(*Pause; then, as if to memorize the words*)
Brute. Beast. Yes?

CHARLIE

Right on.

(*Pause*)

LESLIE

(*Suddenly aware of all eyes on him*)
Stop it! Stop it! What are you looking at? Why don't you mind your own business?

NANCY

What more do you want?

CHARLIE

(*Intense*)

I don't *know* what more I want.

(*To* LESLIE *and* SARAH)

I don't know what I want for *you*. I don't know what I
feel toward you; it's either love or loathing. Take your
pick; they're both emotions. And you're finding out
about them, aren't you? About emotions? Well, I want
you to know about *all* of it; I'm impatient for you. I
want you to experience the whole thing! The full sweep!
Maybe I envy you . . . down *there*, free from it all;
down there with the *beasts?*

(*A pause*)

What would you do, Sarah? . . . if Leslie went away . . .
for a long time . . . what would you do then?

SARAH

If he didn't tell me where he was going?

CHARLIE

If he'd gone!

(*Under his breath*)

For God's sake.

(*Back*)

If he'd taken off, and you hadn't seen him for the
longest time.

SARAH

I'd go look for him.

LESLIE (*Suspicious*)

What are you *after*?

CHARLIE

(*To* SARAH; *ignoring* LESLIE)
You'd go look for him; fine. But what if you knew he
was never coming back?
(SARAH *does a sharp intake of breath*)
What about that?

NANCY

You're heartless, Charlie; you're relentless and without
heart.

CHARLIE (*Eyes narrowing*)

What would you do, Sarah?
(*A pause, then she begins to sob*)

SARAH

I'd . . . I'd . . .

CHARLIE

You'd cry; you'd cry your eyes out.

SARAH

I'd . . . cry; I'd . . . I'd cry! I'd . . . I'd cry my eyes out!
Oh . . . Leslie!

LESLIE

(*Trying to comfort* SARAH)

It's all right, Sarah!

SARAH

I want to go back; I don't want to stay here any more.

(*Wailing*)

I want to go *back!*

(*Trying to break away*)

I want to go *back!*

NANCY

(*Moves to* SARAH, *to comfort her*)

Oh, now, Sarah! Please!

SARAH

Oh, Nancy!

(*Bursts into new sobbing*)

I want to go back!

NANCY

Sarah!

CHARLIE

I'm sorry; I'm . . . I'm sorry.

LESLIE

Hey! Mister!

(Hit)

You've made her cry; she's never done anything like that.

(Hit)

You made her cry!

(Hit)

CHARLIE

I'm sorry, I . . . stop that!
I'm sorry; I . . .

(Hit)

. . . stop that!

LESLIE

You made her cry!

(Hit)

CHARLIE

STOP IT!

LESLIE

I ought to tear you apart!

CHARLIE

Oh my God!
(LESLIE *begins to choke* CHARLIE, *standing be-*
hind CHARLIE, *his arm around* CHARLIE's *throat.*
It has the look of slow, massive inevitability,
not fight and panic)

NANCY

Charlie!

> (SARAH *and* NANCY *rush to stop it*)

SARAH

Leslie! Stop it!

CHARLIE

Stop . . . it . . .

LESLIE

> (*Straining with the effort*)

You . . . made . . . her . . . cry . . . mister.

NANCY

Stop! Please!

SARAH

Leslie!

CHARLIE (*Choking*)

Help . . . me . . .

> (LESLIE *suddenly lets go;* CHARLIE *sinks to the sand*)

LESLIE

Don't you talk to me about brute beast.

SARAH *(To* LESLIE*)*

See to him.

LESLIE *(Cold)*

Are you all right?

CHARLIE

Yes; yes, I am.

(Pause)

LESLIE

(Attempts a quiet half joke)
It's . . . rather dangerous . . . up here.

CHARLIE

(Looks him in the eye)
Everywhere.

LESLIE

Well. I think we'll go back down now.

NANCY

(Hand out; a quiet, intense supplication)
No!

LESLIE

Oh, yes. I think we must.

NANCY

No! You mustn't!

SARAH (*As a comfort*)

Leslie says we must.
                    (*Leslie puts his paw out*)

NANCY

No!
                    (CHARLIE *takes it*)

LESLIE

This *is* how we do it, isn't it?

SARAH (*Watching; tentative*)

Such a wonderful thing to want to do.

LESLIE (*Tight; formal*)

Thank you very much.

NANCY

No!

CHARLIE (*Eyes averted*)

You're welcome.

NANCY

NO!

LESLIE (*Sighs*)

Well.
> (LESLIE *and* SARAH *start moving up to the up-stage dune to exit*)

NANCY (*In place*)

Please?
> (NANCY *moves to follow them*)

SARAH

It's all right; it's all right.

NANCY

You'll have to come back . . . sooner or later. You don't have any choice. Don't you know that? You'll have to come back up.

LESLIE (*Sad smile*)

Do we?

NANCY

Yes!

LESLIE

Do we have to?

NANCY

Yes!

LESLIE

Do we *have* to?

NANCY (*Timid*)

We could *help* you. Please?

LESLIE (*Anger and doubt*)

How?

CHARLIE (*Sad, shy*)

Take you by the hand? You've got to *do* it—sooner or later.

NANCY (*Shy*)

We *could* help you.
>   (LESLIE *pauses; descends a step down the dune; crouches; stares at them*)

LESLIE (*Straight*)

All right. Begin.

CURTAIN

EDWARD ALBEE

Edward Albee was born March 12, 1928, and began writing plays thirty years later. His plays are, in order of composition: *The Zoo Story; The Death of Bessie Smith; The Sandbox; The American Dream; Who's Afraid of Virginia Woolf?; The Ballad of the Sad Cafe* (adapted from Carson McCuller's novella); *Tiny Alice; Malcolm* (adapted from James Purdy's novel); *A Delicate Balance; Everything in the Garden* (adapted from a play by Giles Cooper); *Box and Quotations from Chairman Mao Tse-Tung; All Over;* and *Seascape.*